Junius E. Wharton

The Sun-God

An Indian Edda from the Mythology and Traditional Lore of the

Sun-Worshiping Indians

Junius E. Wharton

The Sun-God
An Indian Edda from the Mythology and Traditional Lore of the Sun-Worshiping Indians

ISBN/EAN: 9783744742429

Printed in Europe, USA, Canada, Australia, Japan

Cover: Foto ©Lupo / pixelio.de

More available books at **www.hansebooks.com**

THE

Sun-God.

An Indian Edda

From the Mythology and Traditional Lore
of the Sun-Worshiping Indians.

BY J. E. WHARTON.

PHŒNIX, ARIZ.:
Published by "Herald" Power Printing House.
1889.

CONTENTS

Introduction.

In this bright clime I have a friend,
A chieftain, very wise and old;
Oft' together, we hours spend
In ancient lore—This tale he told
About his Sun-God's wondrous power;
The source of heat, and light, and force,
And life, and time, for every hour
Is counted by the Sun's bright course.

He told me how the world began,
Thrown from the Sun's great molten sea.
And was prepared for birth of man,
And of its God the Zaptor-Zee.
And how earth's life when it is done,
Shall melt within the Sun's great sea,
All dross burned out, for in the Sun
Is heat, and light, and purity.
And this chief truth he bade me know,
"That heat alone gives light and force;
That naught exists without its glow,
For 'tis of life, the only source.
That heat alone makes light and power,
And on these three all life depends.

Take heat away and at that hour,

On all that's living, death attends.

Yet death is naught for to the Sun,

Our every vital spark shall fly,

And when our earthly race is done,

The Sun-God guides us with His eye,

For in His sight there's nothing lost.

He watches all within His bound,

The smallest spark though tempest tost,

Safe in Sun's sea, will yet be found."

The Creation.

———

" 'Twas many thousand moons, before
The first man ever had been born,
The Sun God stooped and upward bore,
A molten mass from Sun's sea torn.
He hurled it forth past farther star,
Then watched and marked its bound.
The fiery ball returned, and far
Beyond the Sun, again came round.

The Sun-God saw the shining shower,
Half bended like a warrior's bow.
Then by his will and magic power,
He made the world in circle go,
Yet steady, by his power bound
As Sun-God wills, it keeps its place,
And speedy makes each circling round.
While whirling through the awful space,
The thin air on it densely pressed,
And much by heat, to vapor turned,
In water fell upon its breast,
While thunders roared and lightnings burn
So seas were made and rivers broad,
Ran o'er the black scorched land;

Just as our mighty strong Sun-God,

Had in his wisdom planned.

Then cold condensed and warmed by Sun,

The crust breaks into finer mold,

Prepared the ground and then begun

The work of His Sun children bold.

For in earth's centre, Zinktor-Zun,

Ruled by the Earth-God Zaptor-Zee,

Live where the molten rivers run,

Into a fiery molten sea.

Their labor was like childhood's glee,

Above their little sparks they threw,

Up from their bright and molten sea;

Then plants and animals, in view,

Rise living, every herb and tree.

By pairs the animals arise,

Of every kind, each finds its food,

For everything beneath the skies,

By Sun-God planned is very good.

The plants and trees and flowers bloom,

To them the Sun gives color bright,

For everything He giveth room,

Must take its hue from His Sun light.

He shows this in His bow so grand,

That roundly on the clouds He bends,

From this grand bow, on all the land,

His shades of color bright descends.

We see it on the leaves of trees,

And every graceful flower;
So we do find all things to please,
In Sun's heat, light and power.
And lest we may remember ill
Immortal, we to Sun shall fly,
Unsightly worms all dead and still,
In beauty rise and float on high.
And when in winter all is dead,
Each leaf, and plant, and flower,
The light and heat from His great head
In Spring, destroys death's power.
And every night the Sun goes down
In western waves of Death's great Sea,
When morning comes His glorious crown

From Sea of Life comes bright-and free.

So death is nothing, life doth rise

Each day beneath the Sun-God bright,

And all of life beneath the skies

Is part of Him, His life and light.

Earth hath its life from Sun-God given,

For heat is life, and light and force,

And everything that's under heaven

Has life alone from Sun-God's source."

Origin of Man.

"Far in the north, 'neath frozen sky,
There is a cavern grand and vast,
Where icy mountains tower high,
So cold and bleak, no man hath passed,
Nor can endure.   There is the gate
Where Zinktor-Zun have entered in;
Where Zaptor-Zee did watch and wait
command, his labors to begin.

The shining Sun-God from his throne,

The signal makes, that night the north

Gave Zaptor's light, its bright beams shone

To southern sky, swift gleaming forth;

In colors white, that change to red

Were these, the sparks that first made man,

When Zaptor-Zee rais'd high his head.

And as this light o'er earth's face ran,

Up rose the forms of men all strong,

Up rose the forms of women fair;

And so their race they might prolong,

There was of each a living pair.

Nearest the north the white men grow,

A cunning, hardy, crafty race;

They get their hearts from breath of snow.

While southward is the red men's place.

Each race doth have its color true,

From sparks thrown out by Zaptor-Zee;

For in the north the white sparks flew.

The red sparks fell by southern sea.

And now the world was full of life,

And chief of all this life was man,

He ruled the wild beasts in their strife,

Saw, but knew not the Sun-God's plan.

So life to men was wondrous strange,

They do as do the beasts around,

And learn their passions fitful change.

In love and mirth they first abound,

And then in madness, rude and fierce,
They shed each other's blood—the cries
Of tortured victims that they pierce,
Soon reached the Sun-God in the skies.
And then He veiled His face—The gloom
Roused Zaptor-Zee, who looking forth,
Saw Sun-God's signal for man's doom,
And angry lights blazed in the north."

The Great Flood.

"Then Zaptor-Zee in towering height,
Lifts up an icy mountain vast,
And bowed in all his strength of might,
And forth the heavy burden cast.
So great the strain of Earth-God grand,
The world was shaken from its trail,
And now the seas swept all the land,
And few were left to tell the tale.

But where that icy mountain fell,
Tezpi and sons, with wives did gain
The mighty raft, and floated well,
Till landed on a level plain.
Then back into the mighty seas,
The flood's vast waters quickly ran,
All living dead, save only these,
Who should renew the race of man,
And now again the Zinktor-Zun,
Ruled by the Earth-God Zaptor-Zee,
Where streams of molten metal run,
Into earth's central molten sea;
Up through the earth their life sparks send,
Up through the land and in the seas;

These quickly all the life do mend,

Revive the flowers, plants and trees;

They do their work with playful whim;

The animals now all arise,

While in the sea great fishes swim,

And song birds trill throughout the skies.

And Tezpi, with his sons and wives,

Beneath the Sun-God's cheerful light,

Renew'd man's race, and each one strives

To learn and know the heavens bright;

To learn and know the Sun-God's plan.

And what is ill, and what is right,

And all things best, in life, for man."

The Evil Spirit.

——————

"Then came a demon black as night,
From where no Sunlight ever streams,
The Evil One who hides from light,
Where never falls the Sun's bright beams.
To men he brings but sin and crime,
Seeks but to make their labor vain,
Makes bad their hearts with poison slime
And tries to break the Sun-God's reign.

His victims, mad with passions burn,
Drives all that's good in them away,
All sweets to bitter in them turn,
Man's vital spark he seeks to slay.

———

In later years your tribe has brought,
This Evil One to us more strong,
And have our tribe great trouble wrought,
And done us grievous shame and wrong.
He is your fire-water fiend,
That so excites bad passions wild,
And much the red man has demeaned,

His love, and home, and life defiled.

Promotes each wicked, sinful scheme;

Will make a mother slay her child;

And turns sweet sleep to demon's dream.

So many of my tribe—Woe's me!

Have fallen by this poison'd draft,

That few are left on earth to see,

Which God shall break this demon's shaft."

Zunna.

"For many moons my people sought,
A warmer home than frozen north,
And gath'ring all their toil had brought,
On southward trail they journey'd forth;
And many fell along the way,
By mountain demons killed, while some
From sickness died, and day by day,
They weaker grew, ne'er reaching home.

Till all were dead and gone, save one—
Our mother, Zunna, beauteous maid;
Most favored daughter of the Sun,
Here in this valley, weary strayed,
And here on sylvan boughs she found
The sweetest fruit by Sun-God made
To save his love.   Here on the ground
She laid for rest, her charms displayed.
The Sun-God saw her good and pure,
Knelt down and from His loving eyes
His magic cast—she slept secure.
How long she lay the Sun's loved prize,
She never knew.   The balmy air
She softly breathed, and had sweet dreams,

Of lovely lands and views so fair,

Of summer vales and laughing streams;

And lover with a golden crown,

Who to her sued on bended knees,

And at her feet low bowing down,

Strove in sweet words his suit to please.

He seemed a young man wondrous fair,

With flowing hair and sun-bright eyes,

Transported with a love so rare,

She yields herself a willing prize

And then the time so swiftly flew,

In love and joy—There seemed no night

Could ever shade the skies so blue,

Blest by such love, 'mid scenes so bright.

At last the Sun-God bade her rise,

From her long dream of love and joy;

She woke, and with a glad surprise,

Found by her side a girl and boy.

These Zunna loved with mother's care,

And nursed and taught them all she knew,

Of arts of peace and wiles of war;

And when they man and woman grew,

The Sun-God bow'd one glowing day

And straightway to His home above,

He took fair Zunna, there to stay,

Nor let death mar His chosen love."

The Sun Tribe.

"From these Sun children all my tribe
Were born, so plainly you may see,
Why we to Sun-God do ascribe,
Heat, light, force, life and purity;
For we His children knowing more,
Than those less favor'd e'er can know.
How Father's sunbeams on us pour,
And make with life our pulses glow.

And how this land where Zunna dwelt,

Is man's best home, on earth most fair;

For here the Sun Himself hath knelt,

In love unto our mother rare,

And here the Sun keeps lightest day,

And sheds His brightest beams;

Olouds rare obscure His loving ray,

O'er Arizona's vales and streams,"

"And here for many, many years
Our fathers lived and toil'd and died.
They built great towns and had no fears
Of demons from the mountain's side;
They had grand temples for the Sun
And daily worship always paid;
Had great ways built for waters' run;
Broad fields rich harvests yearly made.
The tribe was many thousands strong,
And in its strength grew rich and proud,
And let vile passions rule it wrong,
Till Sun-God in His anger bowed.
Then from the mountains demons came,
And quickly spread in mighty bands

And thousands slew, scarce left a name

Of Sun-Tribe on fair Zunna's lands;

They burned our homes and temples down,

Filled up and dried our water ways,

And made the land a desert brown;

Dead seemed all love in Sun-God's rays.

These mountain demons were unlike

All others unto Sun-Tribe known,

So tall and strong, could death blows strike,

At every stroke, with ax of stone.

Our arrows fell all harmless down,

From armor made of bison hide;

And so they slew in every town,

Till Sun-Tribe's braves all fled or died;

And women, children, but a few
Escaped to other lands again,
To seek and make a home anew,
By sea-shore, or on southern plain.
My band then driven far to west,
Found refuge by a river broad,
But strongly still by demons pressed,
No temple built to great Sun-God;
And so they lived for weary years,
And weak and weaker have they grown
In toil and trouble, pain and fears,
Till Sun-God's worship scarce is known.
At last a tribe in friendship bound
Itself unto our little band,

And then returning we have found,

A home again in Zunna's land.

But never shall we see again

The great Sun temples standing high,

They now are mounds upon the plain,

But Sun·God still doth rule the sky.

Our rites are few, we have no priest,

Yet every morn at Sun-Tribe homes,

Our people watch the lighting east

To see if Moktezuma comes."

Moktezuma.

***

"You tell me from your book that talks,
How your great God His Son did send,
To live awhile in earthly walks,
And for us all, His life did end;
How He hath saved us by His blood,
And taught us all to make life pure,
I listened, for the lore is good,
All's good that makes the spark secure.

Our Sun-God too, to us did send
Great Moktezuma, His own Son;
He was the Sun-Tribe's best, best friend,
And taught us how all things were done;
He showed us how to form the bow,
And make the feathered arrow shaft,
And how to meet our mountain foe,
With all the hunter's wily craft.
He learned us how to turn the mold,
And brought us maize and trego seed,
And built the ke-je, grain to hold,
As food for all in winter's need.
And bade us always have supply,
For twelve full moons when harvest comes.

So that no season cold or dry,

Should famine make in tribal homes.

He learned us how to make survey,

And have the waters outward flow,

From mountain streams, and so make way

For moisture, that our crops might grow.

The mescal plant he showed and taught,

How sweetest food from it is made,

And how its juice fermented brought

Men passions wild, and havoc played.

He showed to us the compass plant,

So we might never wand'ring lose

The trail, and die in famished want.

He taught the games that us amuse,

And made the play of tossing sticks,
And taught young men to throw the ball
From off the foot—and simple tricks
In time of rest, to please us all.
Told each young man to choose a friend,
And to him ever faithful be,
And if their lives they purely spend,
From every wrong completely free;
Good spirits shall between them go,
Though far apart they chance to roam,
They ev'ry day shall surely know
If good or ill to each has come.
He learned the women how to weave
Their webs of bark, and baskets neat,

How rear the children they conceive,

And make the home life pure and sweet.

The clay he showed them to anneal,

And ollas make for every use,

And made metats to grind the meal,

And taught them every artless ruse,

To make their lovers love them well;

So peace and comfort in each home,

Where any of our tribe shall dwell,

He'll find again when he shall come.

He taught our priests their worship grand,

And laid the first great altar stone,

And iztli, shaped by his own hand,

Made sacrificial rites first known.

(You shake your head at this—take heed.

Your rite was worse by far than ours,

While yours did make a God to bleed,

We, with men, best serv'd His powers.

You say for sin blood must atone,

And pardon brings to you and I;

Clean seems the Sun-tribe's altar stone,

To yours, who caused God's Son to die.)

Ere Moktezuma's work was done,

He showed us where the temple stood,

And how the shrine of God the Sun,

On eastern top, is built of wood,

And at the northeast corner stands.

The bloody shrine of God of War,

For from that quarter demon bands

Have always come our homes to mar.

And on the northern rim shall stand,

The shrine of Zaptor, God of Earth.

And at the west, dear to our band.

Zunna's, God's love, who gave us birth.

And at the south a shrine be placed,

For Zinktor-Zun, who gave the fields,

The fruitful life, that hath them graced

And all the charm the earth-mold yields.

That willing victims give the heart

Alone on Sun-God's holy shrine;

And when their sparks to Him depart,

May tell how fares it with our line,

That captives taken by war's art,

Should make the War-God's face to shine;

When from their breasts we tear their hearts

And place them on his bloody shrine,

These held and slain by priestly force,

Upon the round black altar stone,

So made to quit their evil course,

And for their crimes in blood atone;

Before the Earth-God fruits shall lie,

The chosen best of every kind,

And flowers sweet of rarest dye.

Will Zunna's love to maidens bind;

And on the shrine of Zinktor-Zun,

Place fruits and blossoms fresh and fair,

To please these children of the Sun,

Who made them grow so rich and rare.

He bade that on the temple fair,

No idols ever should arise;

That all our worship grand and rare.

Should be the Gods above the skies.

He told us wizards to destroy,

And all that work by demon's charms,

So they the tribe may not annoy,.

By any craft, to make us harm.

He told us how to know them well,

How flames do from their nostrils pour;

And how they make dumb beasts to swell,

The crops to blast, while sick and sore

Our maidens pine, or children wan,
In fever burn, or kill our kine.
That all such demons outward ran,
Be slain beyond the tribal line.
And then he taught us all the law,
That should the tribe together hold,
How strife should cease, and any flaw
Lots should decide, nor love grow cold.
He taught us what things were unclean,
And bade us very careful be,
That nothing sordid, vile or mean,
The Sun-God's eye should ever see,
Lest He might veil His loving face,.
And then disease or famine send

Or Signal Earth-God in his place,
Again man's life by flood to end.
That bloody issues are unclean,
And every woman so bestrait,
If child she has the child must wean,
And from the tribe must outward wait
Till issue cease, and when the Sun
Shines clear on her, at early morn
Must bathe in stream—Her illness done,
Returning then her lodge adorn.
That woman shall court her own love
And ask the man to make her wife,
And if unchaste she ever prove
The man may maim, or take her life.

And when a warrior a man kills—

Though mountain demon—he must bide

Away from tribe, and hide in hills

Till the clear Sun, in morning ride

The eastern sky, and shining bright,

Then lave in stream, he may return

All clean and pure in Sun-God's sight,

To where his lodge's fires burn.

That doctors should be men of skill;

If many die from fell disease,

The Gods have seen their lives are ill;

The tribe to save and Gods to please,

We must at once the doctors slay;

Let others learn and take their place

But have them know that always they

Must surely die, or save the race.

He taught us that no vital spark,

By fault of us be kept away,

Or held by force in shadows dark,

Hid from the Sun-God's light of day.

So bade us all the dead to burn,

As soon as life in them goes out,

So that to Sun they may return;

And that night's darkness we must rout,

By fires bright for thirty nights,

Upon the mounds, where we have laid

Their ashes 'neath—so that the lights

May guide them thro' the earth's dark shade.

He bade us too, this rite to give
E'en to the foe, in battle slain;
For Sun-God gave the spark to live
And to him it must come again.
He made the sacred fire burn
Which must be bright on temple dome,
To greet him when he shall return
To take us to the Sun-God's home.
Far in the southland there's a stone,
Great Moktezuma planned and made
To show us how the time had flown,
And how the earth from path had swayed.
He said at last within the Sun,
All dross burn'd out, pure we shall be,

Our Sun-God's children, Zinktor-Zun,
And there no night shall ever see.
Then from the earth he went away,
Up to his Father's sunlit home;
And when the Sun-God sets the day,
He unto us again will come."

———

"When Moktezuma went to Sun,
He bade us count each passing year,
When five times ten and two are done;
At one such term the end is near.
And on the night the tale is told,
A victim dies at Sun-God's shrine,

No light must burn, all dark and cold,

E'en Sacred Fire must not shine.

If on the morn the Sun rise bright,

We know the time is not yet come,

The Sacred Flame anew we light,

And feasts are spread in every home."

End of the World.

"The fathers told how Sun-God grand,
In mighty power made the world;
And how thrown out by His strong hand,
Past farther star was swiftly hurled.
And when we see a burning star,
Fly fast on high with fiery trail,
'Tis a new world He's thrown afar,
Which shall repeat the earthly tale.

And then they told the wondrous deeds
Of Zaptor-Zee and Zinktor-Zun;
Who gave earth life to serve all needs,
At signal from the God of Sun.
In the earth's center Zinktor-Zun,
Ruled by the Earth-God Zaptor-Zee,
Live where the molten rivers run,
Into a fiery molten sea.
And in their glee and revelry,
The molten waves do often break,
Upon the shores of that bright sea,
And then the hills and valleys shake.
Sometimes they open mountain top,
And throw the burning lava out,

Or hills upon the valleys drop,

While fiery rivers flow about.

For earth can live, but while the heat

In it shall live, and glow and stay;

No life shall be, no pulse shall beat,

When heat to Sun has passed away.

For heat is light, and force, and life,

And must forever be its meed.

I've marvelled much at white men's strife,

Who make and use the thunder seed,

That sends the bullet to the mark,

Yet see not that 'tis heat and force,

But have your minds so blindly dark,

Unto the light, that shows its course.

And then you make the fiery horse,

That swiftly runs across the land,

Which has in heat the mighty force,

You guard so well with iron band.

And then you stretch the talking wire,

And often see, and note its spark;

Who sees not life within that fire,

His mind indeed is very dark.

Whence comes this light, is not the same

Derived from heat? Then 'tis from Sun;

The Sun makes all the stars of flame,

Their hills to rise, their waters run;

Makes all their growth and keeps it warm;

Makes all that lives in them abound;

Makes sunshine bright, and cloudy storm;
Makes all, rules all the worlds around."

———

"When Zaptor-Zee the mountain threw,
The earth ball left her sun-marked trail,
A little space, but ne'er anew
Can gain her path—the closing tale
From there begins—at every round
A shorter length, so we draw nigh
To Sun's grand sea, with nearer bound.
Yet many thousand moons go by,
Ere earth shall reach that centre bright,
Though each twelve moons a little span

Is won, toward that sea of light,

And as the earth grows cold and wan,

Like aged man, with motion slow,

Though it shall have a shorter trail,

Twelve moons shall always come and go,

Each yearly round, to count the tale,

And when it last, its heat all spent,

It then can have no life or force,

Back to the Sun each spark has went;

The old earth then drops from its course,

And into Sun will quickly fall;

Its sin as dross be burned away,

And there shall wait the future call,

To serve again the God of Day."

Conclusion.

"But since your tribe to us has come,
Gone is the worship of the Sun.
The sacred fire on the dome
Is dead: This yours to us have done.
And many, many moons have gone,
Since victim died on altar stone,
And yet the Sun-God still shines on:
There's only mounds where temples shone.

The Sun-Tribe now is poor and weak,

Gone are its shrines of cedar wood,

But Sun-God yet some day will speak,

For He is great and strong and good.

Mayhap this failing is the sign,

That Moktezuma soon will come,

And that this dying of our line,

Is just before the welcome home.

And yet sometimes it seems to me,

That you and I both seek the same

Great God of life all pure and free;

That while we grope all blind and lame,

Your God of Light, my God of Day;

My Moktezuma—your God's Son,

Are all true lights upon the way,

· By which we seek life's source—the Sun.

Your God, you say, is life and light,

And sin hath brought us death and pain,

And in your Heaven there's no night,

Relieved from sin to die is gain.

Our Sun-God too is life and light,

He sin destroys—then ceases pain;

On Sun's bright face there is no night,

For all is light within His reign.

You speak of Hell that sin destroys,

And all the Evil One hath given

Our Sun burns out all that annoys,

And changes Hell into a Heaven,

For Sun's heat can no dross endure,
No sin is there, no sorrow's blight,
Refined by fire, there all is pure,
'Tis perfect day, 'tis life and light."

"We both are old my white man friend,
And in our world life shall not see
The day when this great world shall end,
Yet we shall meet in Sun's bright sea,
And there immortal Zinktor-Zun,
Both you and I will ever be;
Or if the great God of the Sun

Should wisdom find in you or me,

When a new world shall outward run,

He may choose one for Zaptor-Zee;

And if on you that choice should fall,

When hurled in space by mighty Sun,

With you I'll ride the fiery ball,

A bright, immortal Zinktor-Zun."

NOTES.

NOTES.

THE SUN-GOD—In writing this I have used the mythology and traditions of the River Indians of Arizona. There is quite a difference in the manners, laws and customs of these River Indians as compared to the hill or mountain tribes. They appear to be a remnant of the ancient Aztecs and claim a mythology and traditions many centuries preceding the conquest of Mexico.

PAGE 8. *And of its God the Zaptor-Zee.*

I have not pretended to give the unpronouncable names of the Indian deities. The Zaptor-Zee is the *Aurora Borealis* of the north.

PAGE 13. *Their labor was like childhood's glee.*

All nations seem to have their little people in their lore. The creation of many things, to the Indian mind appears childish and whimsical.

PAGE 15. *In western waves of Death's great sea.*
As the setting sun appears to be drowned in the Pacific Ocean, it is called by the Indians the Sea of Death, while the Atlantic from which it rises in the morning, is called the Sea of Life. Among the sun-worshipers peculiar virtues are believed to exist in the waters of the Sea of Life which they use, when obtainable, in some of their religious rites.

PAGE 22. *Tezpi and sons with wives did gain.*
This tradition prevails among the southern Indians and they generally use the name Tezpi as that of the head of the family which was saved from the Deluge.

PAGE 27. *On southward trail they journeyed forth.*
All the sun-worshiping Indians claim to have migrated, many centuries ago, from the northwest.

PAGE 27. *By mountain demons killed.*
This is English for what the River Indians call the hostile tribes, especially the Apaches.

PAGE 28. *Our mother, Zunna, beanteous maid.*
The story of Zunna (pronounced Zoon-nah) is given in accordance with the claims of the River Indians of Arizona.

PAGE 28. *The sweetest fruit by Sun-God made.*

This refers to the mesquit bean which grows on the mesquit, a species of the acacia tree in Arizona. From the pods of these beans the Indians grind a meal that is very sweet and nutritious.

PAGE 32. *O'er Arizona's vales and streams.*

As none of the ruins of the great sun temples are found north of Arizona and as all the traditions of the Aztecs claim that they migrated from the northwest it is plain that Arizona was the scene of Zunna's life and Moktezuma's labors. Bancroft Library

PAGE 34. *They burned our homes.*

Evidence of destruction by fire is generally found in excavating the pre-historic ruins of Arizona. Charred wood and the burnt ends of cedar beams, still sticking in the walls, where walls are standing, attest this fact. The exterminated people in some instances seem to have been taken by surprise while at peaceful avocations. Their remains have been found near cooking vessels containing the bones of animals, these vessels being over the charred remains of a fire, showing that the people were probably killed while preparing their food.

PAGE 34.   *At every stroke with ax of stone.*

Many stone axes are found in and around the ancient ruins of Arizona. As no relics of the Stone Age except such as might be used for weapons are found here, this fact is strongly corroborative of the traditions of this ancient war of extermination.

PAGE 35.   *My band then driven far to west.*

The Maricopa tribe almost exterminated by the ancient wars sought refuge on the lower Colorado river.

PAGE 35.   *At last a tribe in friendship bound.*

The Pima tribe made a treaty of protection with the Maricopas and the latter then removed to the lands where they now live, at the junction of the Salt and Gila rivers in Arizona.

PAGE 38.   *Great Moktezuma, His own Son.*

Moktezuma the great leader and Law-giver of the sun-worshiping Indians must not be mistaken for the Montezuma overcome by Cortez. Moktezuma antedated the conquest of Mexico many centuries.

PAGE 38.   *And brought us maize and trego seed.*

Maize (pronounced mice.) Trego (pronounced tree-go,) is wheat. Of this these Indians raise a superior variety. They claim great antiquity in its introduction; but most probably received the grain first from the Spaniards.

PAGE 38. *And built the ke-je grain to hold.*
The keje (pronounced key-ye) is a round bin built of wicker-work and straw.

PAGE 38. *And bade us always have supply.*
These Indians always keep grain enough for a year in advance, until the pending harvest is assured.

PAGE 39. *He learned us how to make survey.*
The pre-historic irrigating canals of Arizona show that those who made them had some system of surveying. Our engineers can improve but little on the levels of these ancient ditches.

PAGE 39. *The mescal plant he showed and taught.*
The mescal is the century plant. It heads up something like a cabbage for several years before sending up its flower stalk. These heads roasted make a sweet, nutritious food that will sustain life without any other aliment, for long periods. From its juice a strong intoxicant is made.

72 NOTES.

Page 39. *He showed to us the compass plant.*

The compass plant is what is commonly known as "rosin weed" and grows on all praries and plains of the west. While young, its leaves point, in general bearing, north and south.

Page 40. *And made the play of tossing sticks.*

This is an old game of the River Indians and they sometimes gamble desperately on its chances. Sitting in a circle on the ground each player alternately tosses up the bunch of sticks and the game is counted according to the position they happen to take on falling to the ground. .

Page 40. *And taught young men to throw the ball.*

This is a favorite game. The ball is made from gum-shellac obtained from what is commonly called "grease-wood," a shrub that grows plentifully in Arizona. It is thrown from off the foot for a long distance and then there is a foot race to see who will first recover the ball, the winner being entitled to the next throw.

Page 40. *Their webs of bark and baskets neat.*

On the advent of the whites into Arizona the dress of the Indian women was generally a short tunic of woven bark. The baskets made by them are marvels of patient neatness and are so closely woven that they will hold water.

PAGE 41. *And ollas made for every use.*

These Indians make a great amount of porous or unglazed pottery. Their ollas, (pronounced oh-yahs) are made to contain water and for all cooking purposes. Being porous the water sweats through and the evaporation from the outside of such vessels makes the water within, cold in the hottest weather.

PAGE 41. *And made metats to grind the meal.*

The metat is a hand mill with a rubbing or grinding stone, both made of volcanic trap rock.

PAGE 41. *And iztli shaped by his own hand.*

Iztlii is obsidian or volcanic glass. The sacrificial knives and razors of the Aztecs were made of it.

PAGE 42. *On eastern top is built of wood.*

The pre-historic sun temples were built true to the cardinal points of the compass.

PAGE 45. *No idols ever should arise.*

The River Indians claim that their ancestors never worshiped idols. No remains of idols have been found in any pre-historic temple ruin in Arizona.

PAGE 45. *He told us wizards to destroy.*

This practice of killing for witchcraft is still enforced by the sun-worshiping Indians. It is so stated by Indian children who have been adopted into white families. Not many years ago the Maricopas clubbed an alleged wizard to death, within the city limits of Phoenix, Arizona. The Zunis also enforce this law.

PAGE 46. *He taught us what things were unclean.*

In this matter some of the customs of these Indians resemble the usage and laws of the Jews.

PAGE 46. *That nothing sordid, vile or mean.*

Bancroft's "Native Races" gives a translation of a letter from an Aztec parent to a child, that for its teachings of pure morality would be creditable to the enlightenment of our own race.

PAGE 47. *That woman shall court her own love.*

This rule as to courtship and chastity still prevails among the Maricopa and Zuni Indians.

PAGE 48. *We must at once the doctors slay.*

This law is enforced whenever there is any great fatality from an epidemic disease.

PAGE 49. *So bade us all the dead to burn.*

As soon as it is believed that death is inevitable, kindling and combustible material is placed under and about the bed and as soon as death takes place, fire is applied and the body, lodge and all property of the deceased is consumed. The ashes and bones of the dead are then gathered, placed in an olla and buried.

PAGE 50. *He made the Sacred Fire burn.*

This fire was to be kept perpetually burning until Moktezuma's return. The Indians claim that it was so kept during all the years of the sun worship.

PAGE 50. *Far in the southland there's a stone.*

The great calendar stone of the Aztecs. See American Cyclopedia.

PAGE 59. *This yours to us have done.*

That the sun-worshiping Indians cling with remarkable tenacity to their belief was shown in the conquest of Mexico. The Catholics made few converts except by force and only succeeded in becoming paramount by mingling the Spanish blood with the native race. The smaller bands of these Indians who failed to be so united rejected the Romish Church. The Zuni's tolerate Catholicism but retain all their traditional rites except human sacrifice. The Maricopas have never accepted the Catholic or any other Christian teaching.

www.ingramcontent.com/pod-product-compliance
Lightning Source LLC
Chambersburg PA
CBHW022145090426

42742CB00010B/1400